PIANO / VOCAL / GUITAR

TOP HITS OF 2010

ISBN 978-1-4234-9958-9

HAL•LEONARD®
CORPORATION
7777 W. BLUEMOUND RD. P.O. BOX 13819 MILWAUKEE, WI 53213

Visit Hal Leonard Online at
www.halleonard.com

AIRPLANES

Words and Music by BOBBY RAY SIMMONS JR.,
ALEXANDER GRANT, JEREMY DUSSOLLIETY,
TIM SOMMERS and JUSTIN FRANKS

Moderate Hip-Hop groove

Can we pre-tend that air-planes in the night sky are like shoot-in' stars? __ I could real-ly use a wish right now, __ wish right now, __ wish right now. __ Can we pre-tend that air-planes in the night sky are like

Can we pre-tend that

air - planes _ in the night sky _ are like shoot-in' stars? _ I could real-ly use a

Additional Lyrics

Rap 1:   Yeah, I could use a dream or a genie or a wish to go back to a place much simpler than this.
'Cause after all the partyin' and smashin' and crashin', and all the glitz and the glam and the fashion,
And all the pandemonium and all the madness, there comes a time where you fade to the blackness.
And when you starin' at that phone in your lap, and you hopin', but them people never call you back.
But that's just how the story unfolds, you get another hand soon after you fold.
And when your plans unravel in the sand, what would you wish for if you had one chance?
So, airplane, airplane, sorry I'm late. I'm on my way, so don't close that gate.
If I don't make that then I'll switch my flight and I'll be right back at it by the end of the night.
Chorus

Rap 2:   Yeah, yeah, somebody take me back to the days before this was a job, before I got paid.
Before it ever mattered what I had in my bank, yeah, back when I was tryin' to get a tip at Subway.
And back when I was rappin' for the hell of it, but now-a-days we rappin' to stay relevant.
I'm guessin' that if we can make some wishes outta airplanes, then maybe, yo, maybe I'll go back to the days
Before the politics that we call the rap game, and back when ain't nobody listen to my mix tape,
And back before I tried to cover up my slang. But this is for Decatur, what's up Bobby Ray?
So can I get a wish to end the politics and get back to the music that started this sh*t?
So here I stand, and then again I say I'm hopin' we can make some wishes outta airplanes.
Chorus

BAD ROMANCE

Words and Music by STEFANI GERMANOTTA
and NADIR KHAYAT

Moderate Techno groove

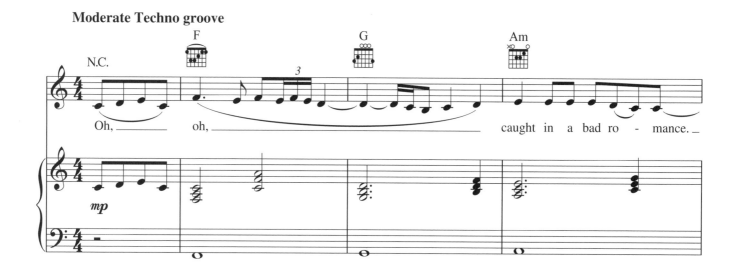

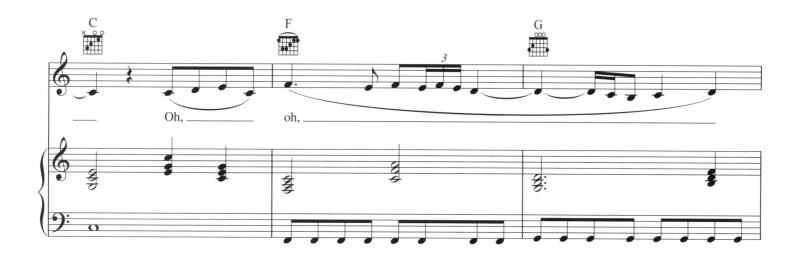

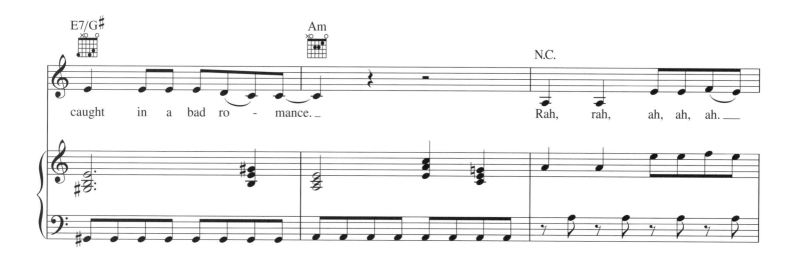

ALEJANDRO

Words and Music by STEFANI GERMANOTTA
and NADIR KHAYAT

Andante rubato

Spoken: "I know that we are young, and I know that you may love me

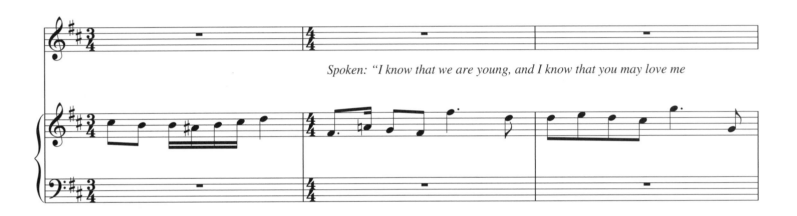

Moderate Pop feel

but I just can't be with you like this anymore, Alejandro."

She's got both hands ___ in her
bro - ken, ___ she's just a ba -

pock - ets
- by

and she ___ won't look at you, ___ won't look at you. ___
but her boy-friend's like a dad, ___ just like a dad. ___

BABY

Words and Music by JUSTIN BIEBER,
CHRISTOPHER STEWART, CHRISTINE FLORES,
CHRISTOPHER BRIDGES and TERIUS NASH

With energy

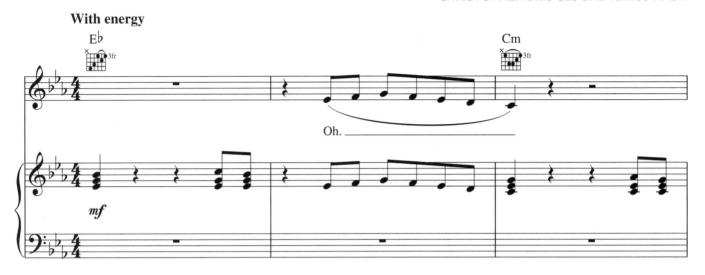

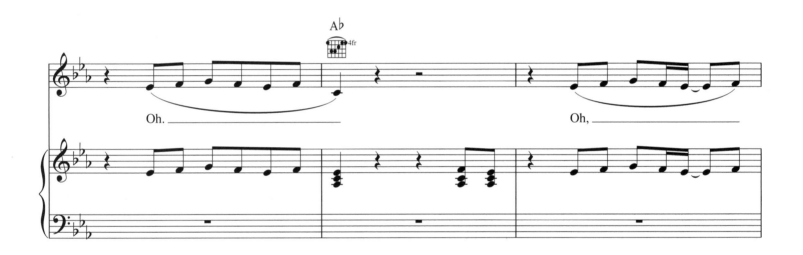

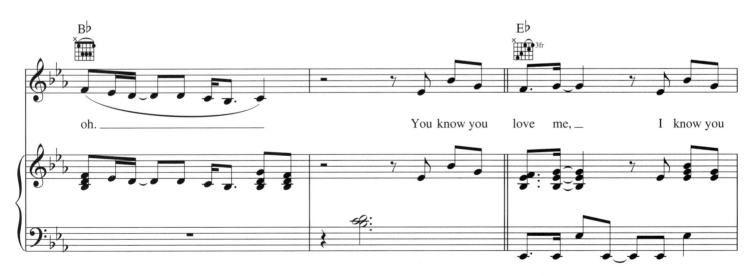

BILLIONAIRE

Words and Music by TRAVIS McCOY,
PHILIP LAWRENCE, BRUNO MARS
and ARI LEVINE

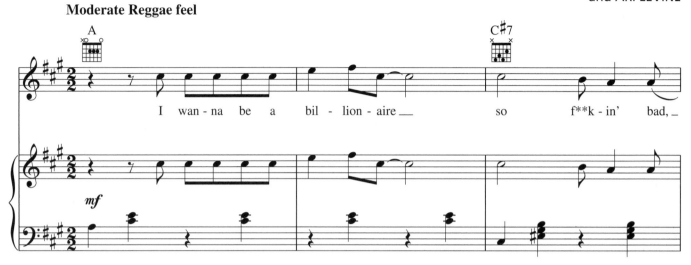

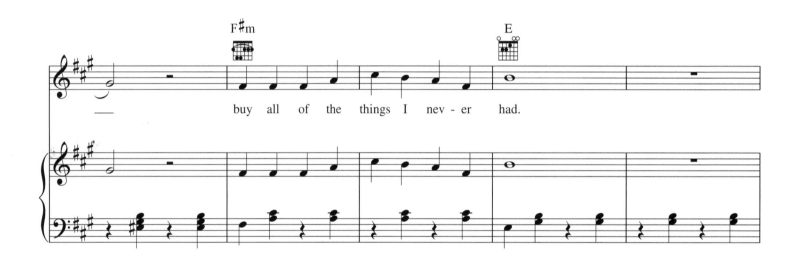

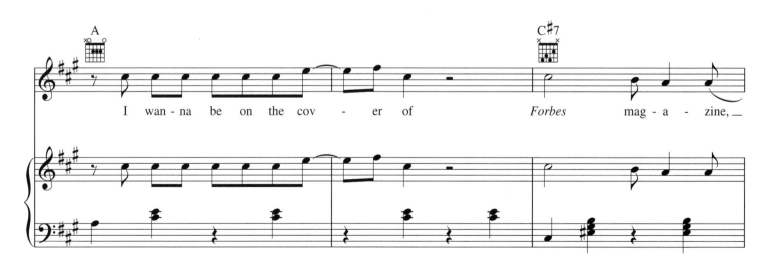

BREAKEVEN

Words and Music by STEPHEN KIPNER,
ANDREW FRAMPTON, DANIEL O'DONOGHUE
and MARK SHEEHAN

Moderate Pop Rock

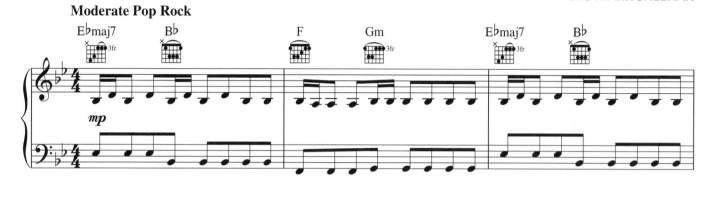

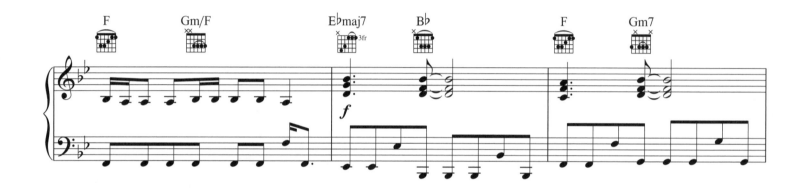

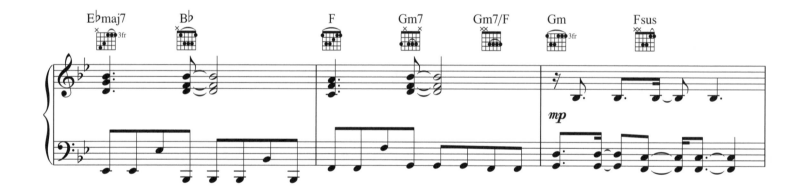

I'm still a-live but I'm bare-ly breath-in',

LIVE LIKE WE'RE DYING

Words and Music by STEPHEN KIPNER,
ANDREW FRAMPTON, DANIEL O'DONOGHUE
and MARK SHEEHAN

Moderate Pop Rock

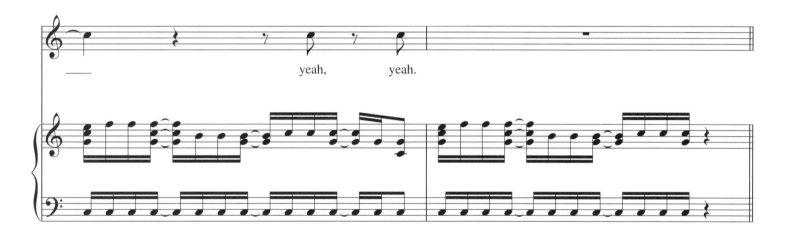

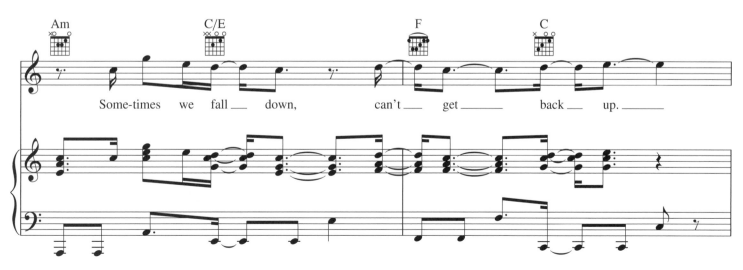

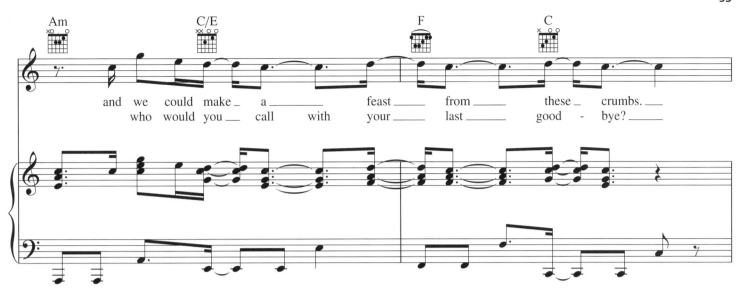

and we could make a _____ feast _____ from _____ these _ crumbs. ___
who would you __ call with your _____ last _____ good - bye? _____

And we're all star - ing down __ the bar - rel _____ of a _____ gun. So if your
Should be so care - ful who we let _____ fall _____ out our _____ lives. When we

life flashed __ be - fore __ you, what would you wish you would have done? __ Yeah, we got - ta start
long for ab - so - lu - tion, there'll be no one on the line. ___ Yeah, we got - ta start

look-ing at the hands of the time we've been giv-en. If this is all we got, then we got-ta start think-in' if

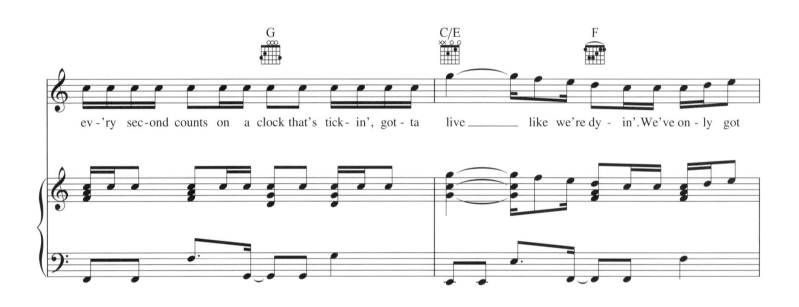

ev-'ry sec-ond counts on a clock that's tick-in', got-ta live _____ like we're dy-in'. We've on-ly got

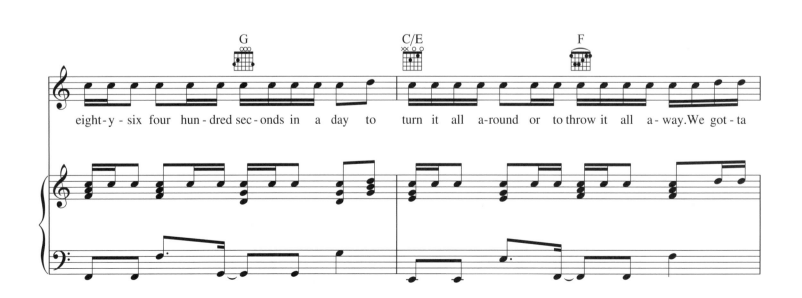

eight-y-six four hun-dred sec-onds in a day to turn it all a-round or to throw it all a-way. We got-ta

tell 'em that we love 'em while we got the chance to say, got-ta live ____ like we're dy-in', ____ oh.

live ____ like we're dy-in', ____ oh. Like we're dy-in', ___ oh, _____ like we're dy-in'.

Like we're dy - in', ___ oh, _____ like we're dy - in'. We've on - ly got

CALIFORNIA GURLS

Words and Music by MAX MARTIN,
LUKASZ GOTTWALD, BENJAMIN LEVIN,
CALVIN BROADUS and KATY PERRY

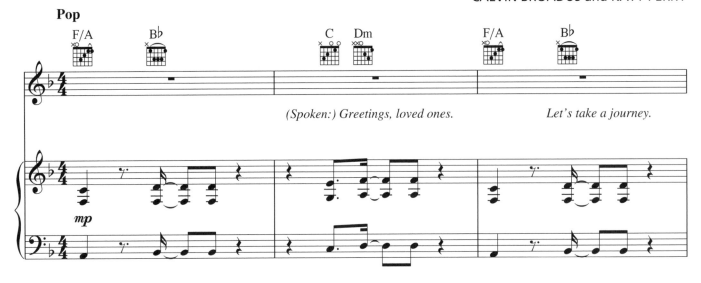

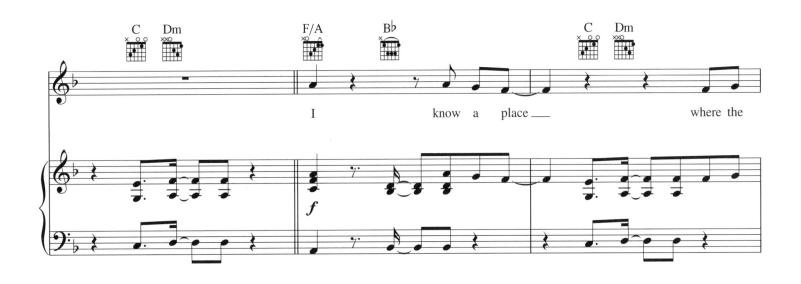

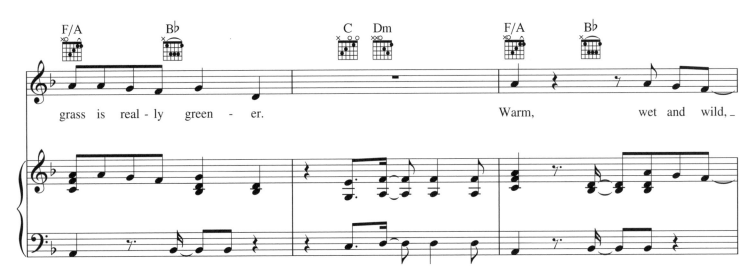

COOLER THAN ME

Words and Music by MIKE POSNER
and ERIC HOLLJES

Moderate Dance groove

If I could write you a song to make you fall in love, I would

al-read-y have you up un-der my arm. I used up all of my tricks. I hope that

you like this, but you prob-a-bly won't. You think you're cool-er than me. You got de-

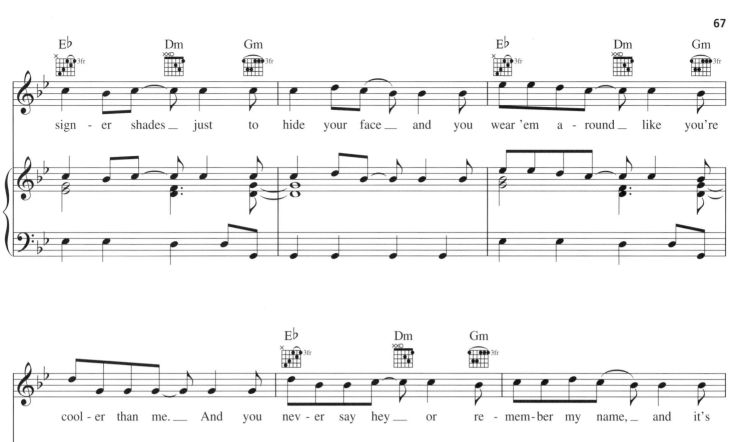

sign - er shades __ just to hide your face __ and you wear 'em a - round __ like you're

cool - er than me. __ And you nev - er say hey __ or re - mem-ber my name, __ and it's

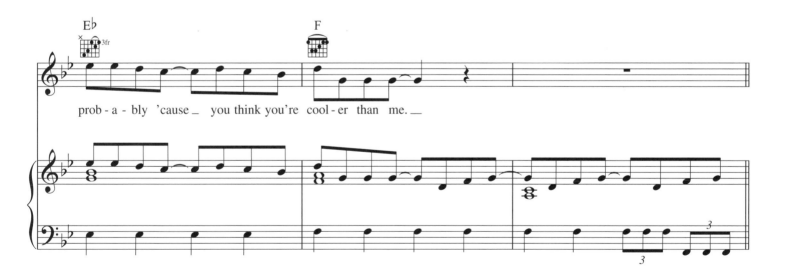

prob - a - bly 'cause __ you think you're cool - er than me. __

Play 3 times

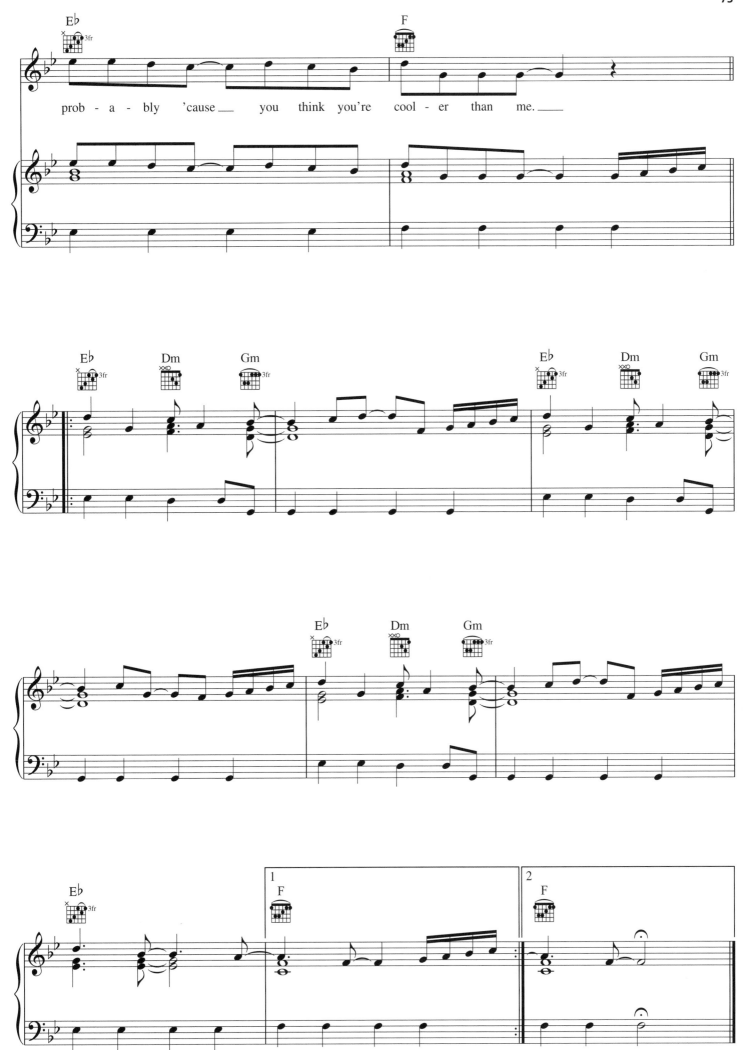

HEY, SOUL SISTER

Words and Music by PAT MONAHAN,
ESPEN LIND and AMUND BJORKLAND

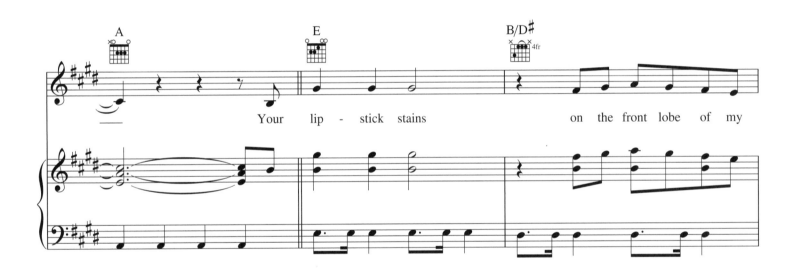

LOVING YOU IS EASY

Words and Music by
SARAH McLACHLAN

TODAY WAS A FAIRYTALE

from VALENTINE'S DAY

Words and Music by
TAYLOR SWIFT

MINE

Words and Music by
TAYLOR SWIFT

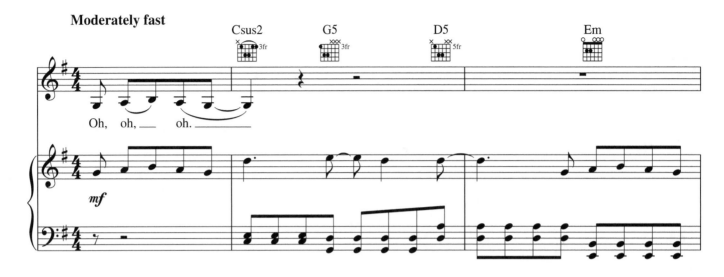

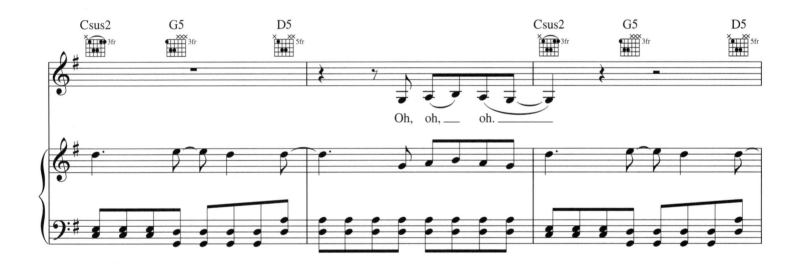

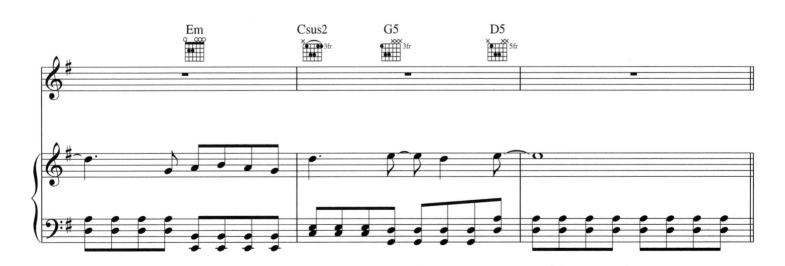

MISERY

Words by ADAM LEVINE
Music by ADAM LEVINE, JESSE CARMICHAEL
and SAM FARRAR

Moderate Funk Rock groove

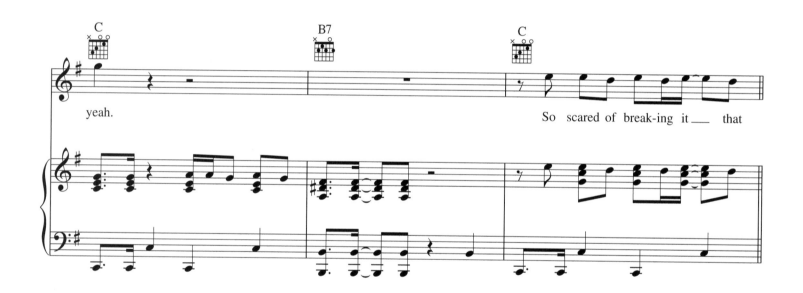

NEED YOU NOW

Words and Music by HILLARY SCOTT,
CHARLES KELLEY, DAVE HAYWOOD
and JOSH KEAR

THERE GOES MY BABY

Words and Music by RICHARD BUTLER,
JAMES SCHEFFER, FRANK ROMANO
and DANIEL MORRIS

Moderate groove

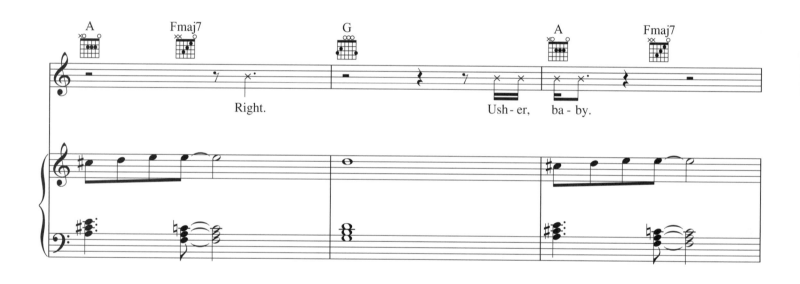

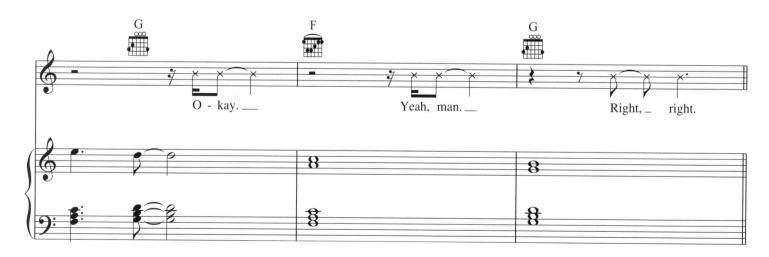

WHEN I LOOK AT YOU

Words and Music by JOHN SHANKS
and HILLARY LINDSEY

YOUR LOVE IS MY DRUG

Words and Music by KESHA SEBERT,
JOSHUA EMANUEL COLEMAN and PEBE SEBERT

* Recorded a half step higher.

WHAT YA WANT FROM ME

Words and Music by ALECIA MOORE,
MAX MARTIN and JOHAN SCHUSTER

Hey, ____ what do you want ____ Hey, ____ what do you want ____

____ from me, what do you want __ from me, what do you want ___ from me? _____ What do you want __

____ from me, what do you want __ from me? _____